Welcome the Stranger

For Bob and Susie Skinner

Copyright © 1984 Concordia Publishing House
3558 S. Jefferson Avenue, St. Louis, MO 63118-3968
Manufactured in the United States of America.

Library of Congress Cataloging in Publication Data

Greene, Carol.
    Welcome the stranger.

    Summary: A retelling of the birth of Jesus using contemporary characters.
    1. Children's stories, American. [1. Jesus Christ—Nativity—Fiction. 2. Christmas—Fiction. 3. Puppets—Fiction] I. Boyanchek, Dave, ill.
II. Title. PZ7.G82845We 1984   [Fic]   84-14941
ISBN 0-570-04105-8

1   2   3   4   5   6   7   8   9   10   DB   93   92   91   90   89   88   87   86   85   84

Welcome the Stranger

by Carol Greene

featuring
Dave Pavelonis' Peppercorn Puppets

photographed by
Herb Halpern and David Boyanchek

Cover photography: Val Gelineau

Publishing House
St. Louis

How cold the wind blew that winter night! The children had traveled a long way, but the wind always followed behind, shoving at their backs and whistling in their ears. The boy shivered and pulled his cloak tighter. The girl stumbled and almost fell. The moon lit the road for them. But the stars were far away and cold as the wind.

"We shouldn't have come," said the girl.

"Hush," said the boy. "You're just hungry. Let's stop and eat our dinner."

"There's no more food," said the girl.

"Then let's stop and rest."

They left the road and sat down.

"We shouldn't have come," said the girl again.

"What else could we do?" asked the boy. "The old country is destroyed by war. Our master's house is gone and so is our master. We couldn't stay there anymore. No one wanted us—a couple of servants with no one to serve."

"Well, no one wants us here either," said the girl.

"Hush." The boy patted her arm. "Maybe someone will. I have a good feeling about this place. It seems to be—well—waiting for something. And haven't you noticed the wind? The way it almost seems to be pushing us in this direction?"

"Don't be silly," sniffed the girl. "Wind is wind. It blows wherever it wants."

"That's what I mean," said the boy. "Why does it want to blow this way all the time? And look at the stars. See how close they've come? It's as if something is about to happen and they want to see too."

The girl glanced up. The stars did seem less cold and far away.

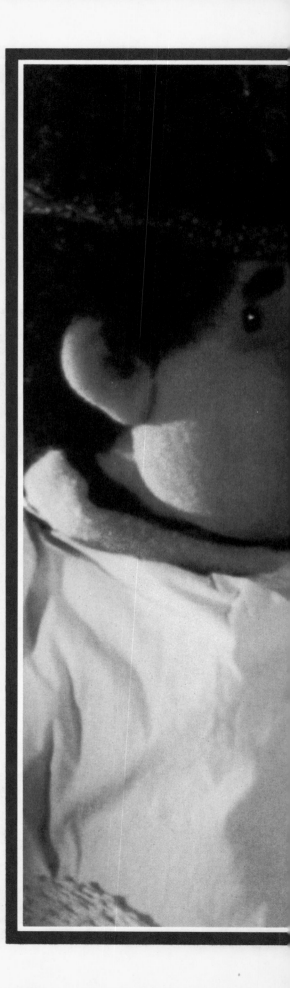

"Come on," said the boy. "I'll sing us a song. Then we'll go on. I'm sure we'll find something to eat in the next town."

"Well—all right." The girl took out her little wooden recorder and began to play. Then the boy began to sing:

"What place is this, this waiting place,
That lies in restless dreaming,
Where starry light through solemn night
A word of hope is beaming?"

They paused, and an instant later heard an echo, silver and clear, as if the stars themselves were singing the answer:

"This, this is Israel,
Whose tale the prophet voices tell.
This, this is a holy place,
The land that God has chosen."

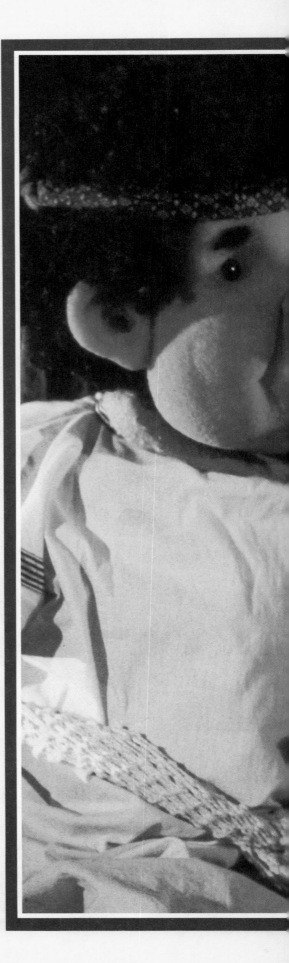

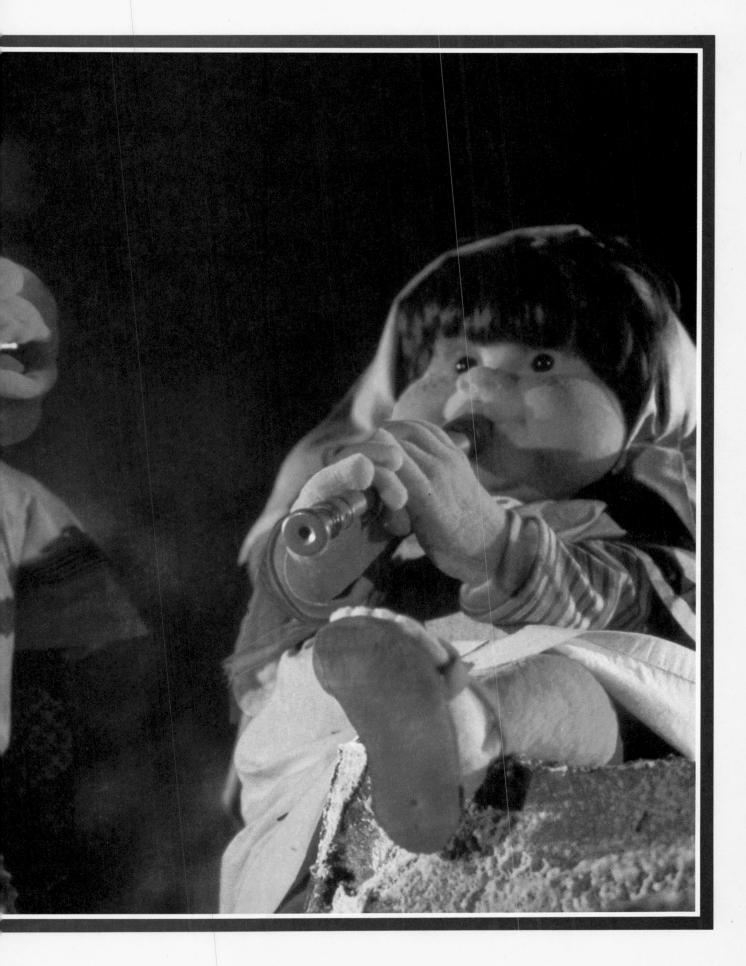

For a moment the children stared at one another. Then the boy began to stammer. "I—I don't understand."

"Neither do I." The girl pulled at his hand. "Let's go on."

So on they went and with each step the stars seemed to grow brighter and the wind less cold. Their road led them up a hill and down, then up another.

"We'd better rest again," panted the boy. "Look, there's still another hill ahead. I don't think we'll ever reach a town."

"Of course we will." The girl sat down on a rock at the edge of the road. "But I wish it would be soon. I'm awfully hungry."

"So am I." The boy sat beside her and together they gazed at the hill ahead. By now the stars shone so bright that they could see sheep milling around on the slopes. One man was trying to quiet them while other men slept on the ground, their shabby cloaks wrapped around them like gray cocoons.

"Even the sheep are restless," said the girl. "I wonder—"

She stopped and caught her breath. All at once the wind had begun to blow very hard, rushing past them, spinning and swirling in golden spirals across the sky. The sleeping men leaped to their feet, then fell to the ground again and covered their faces. And then the whole night exploded into a glorious golden light and a voice, mightier than thunder, but somehow gentle too, began to speak.

"What is it saying?" asked the girl, holding tight to the boy's hand.

"I don't know. I can't tell. The wind is too loud. But listen! There are more voices now. They're singing. Oh, listen! It's the music of heaven."

Tears filled the children's eyes and rolled down their faces as the great glad song swept over them. Then, as quickly as it had come, it was gone and only the stars shone on in the sky.

"Hurry!" cried the girl. "We must ask those men what happened, what the voice said."

"No, wait a minute." The boy held her back. "Let's try something first. Play that song again."

He began to sing:

"What folk are these, these shabby folk,
Whom others have forgotten,
Who shake with fear as sheep draw near
And miracles are begotten?"

His voice sounded small and lonely after the golden song that had just filled the night. But again the stars answered in a clear, silver echo:

"These, these are the shepherd poor,
Whom angel voices reassure.
These, these are the special ones,
The folk whom God has chosen."

"You're right," said the girl softly. "It is a night of miracles."

Together they ran to where the sheep lay, quiet and drowsy now. But all of the men had gone, all but one old shepherd, who leaned on his staff, still looking up at the silent sky.

"Excuse me, sir," said the boy, pulling at the old man's sleeve.

"Yes, yes, what is it?" The shepherd blinked and peered at him as if his eyes could not get used to the dark again.

"We were on that other hill." The boy pointed. "We saw the light and heard the angels' song. But we couldn't hear what the voice said. Would you tell us?"

"Yes, yes. I wondered if anyone else saw and heard. How'd you know they were angels, lad?"

"Why, the stars told me—I think."

The old man rubbed his beard. "Hmf. Maybe they did. Maybe they did. Well, lad, the first one—angel or whatever—told us not to be afraid. Said there was good news for the whole earth, that a Savior was born down in Bethlehem and we'd find Him lying in a manger. Then a lot more of the golden creatures came and sang glory to God and peace on earth. What do you think about that, lad?"

"I—I don't know," said the boy. "But I guess it's a miracle."

The old man nodded. "I guess it is too. Anyway, the others went down to find this baby Savior. They left me behind to watch the sheep."

"But don't you want to go too?" asked the boy.

"I suppose so." The shepherd shrugged. "But when you're as old as I am, you get used to waiting. God promised us a Savior centuries ago. I guess I can hold on a little longer before I see if this really is the one."

"God promised?" The boy glanced at the sky. "I didn't know about that. You see, we come from far away."

The shepherd leaned more comfortably on his staff. "Oh, yes. God promised all right. And one thing's for sure. When God makes a promise, you can count on Him to keep it. That's what the prophets say and they ought to know."

"Prophets?" said the boy.

"Yes, yes. The prophets. You mean you've never heard of them? Folks like Hosea and Jeremiah and that old poet, Isaiah?"

"Well," began the boy, "I think I've *heard* of them, but—"

"Isaiah," said the shepherd with a faraway look on his face. "Yes, yes, he was the one. My favorite. He had a real way with words, Isaiah did. Of course I never met him. He lived hundreds of years ago. But folks still talk about the things he said—the promises God told him."

"Like what?" asked the boy.

"Well, you see, old Isaiah would sit down those people of Israel—my ancestors—and he'd tell them things like: 'Behold, a virgin shall conceive and bear a Son. . . . For unto us a Child is born, unto us a Son is given: and the government shall be upon His shoulder: and His name shall be called Wonderful, Counsellor, the mighty God, the everlasting Father, the Prince of peace.'"

"That's—that's really something!" said the boy.

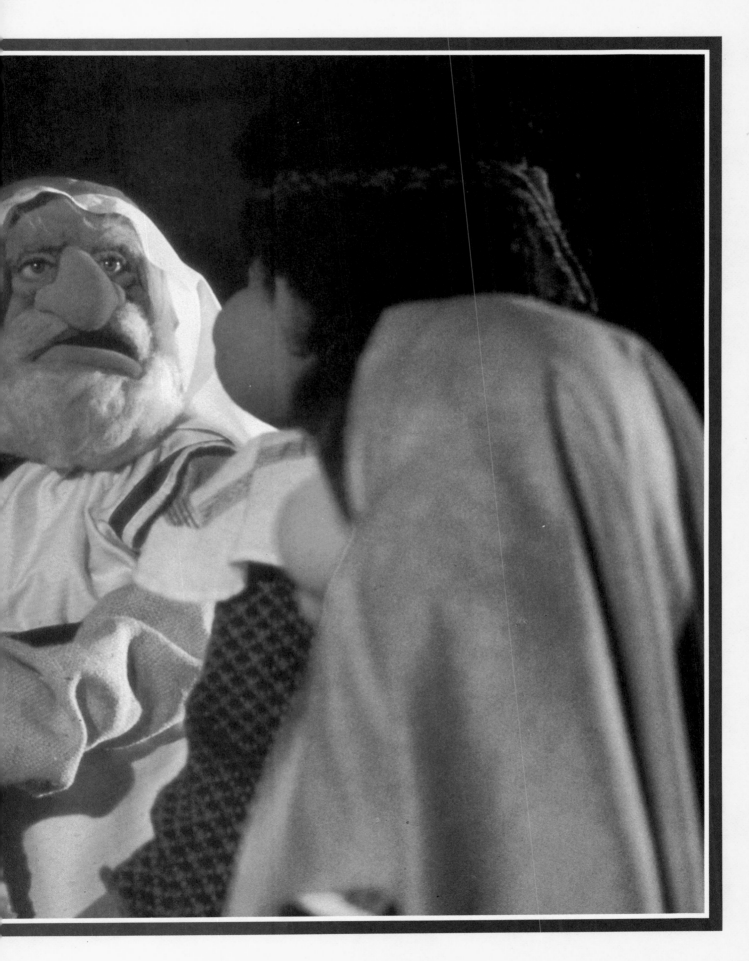

"Oh, yes," agreed the shepherd. "And there were others too. What's the matter with that girl?"

The boy spun around. The girl was sitting on the ground, her head on her knees. She looked up, though, and smiled at him.

"I'm all right. I just got dizzy for a minute."

"She's hungry," said the boy. "We haven't eaten for a long time."

"Well, why didn't you say so?" The old man pointed to a pouch lying on some rocks. "There's bread in there. Take it."

The boy lost no time getting the bread and tearing it into chunks for himself and the girl. Neither of them said a word until the last crumb had been swallowed. Then the girl sighed happily.

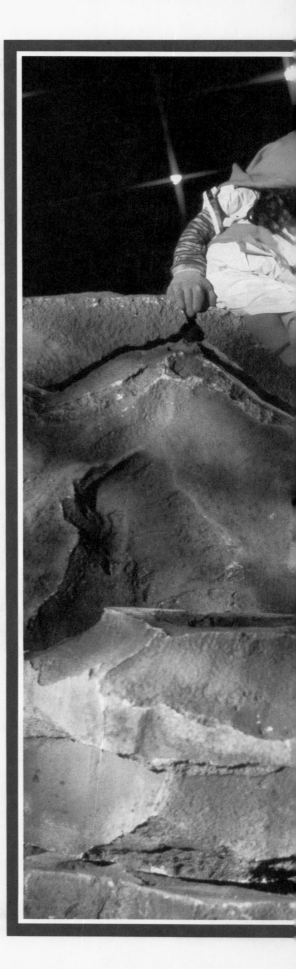

"Thank you," she told the shepherd. "Now won't you let us do something for you? We could watch your sheep while you go see the Baby."

"Never mind the sheep," said the old man. "They aren't going anywhere and nothing's going to bother them—not tonight. There's been enough waiting and watching. We'll all go see the Baby."

He couldn't walk fast and had to lean on his staff with each step. So, even though the wind was pushing behind them again, the children slowed their steps too.

"It must be fun being a shepherd," said the girl to pass the time.

"Fun? Hah!" snorted the old man.

"But isn't it?" she persisted. "You get to be outdoors all the time and play with the little lambs and—and everything."

"You get to be cold and wet and poor. That's what you get to be. You get to break your legs pulling those little lambs out of places they've no business being. And you get to risk your life chasing off wild animals with a wooden staff."

"But don't you like it anyway?" asked the boy.

"Well—yes, I guess I do," the old man admitted. "I've always done it—and my father and grandfather before me. Can't imagine doing anything else. Still, it'd be nice to stay home sometimes. I get lonely for my wife."

"Do you have any children?" asked the girl.

"All grown up and gone. What about you two? You say you come from far away?"

"Yes, sir," said the boy. "We're strangers. We were servants in the same house in another country. Then war broke out. Our master's house was destroyed and our master disappeared. I guess he's dead. There wasn't much point in our staying there anymore. So we set out and—and here we are."

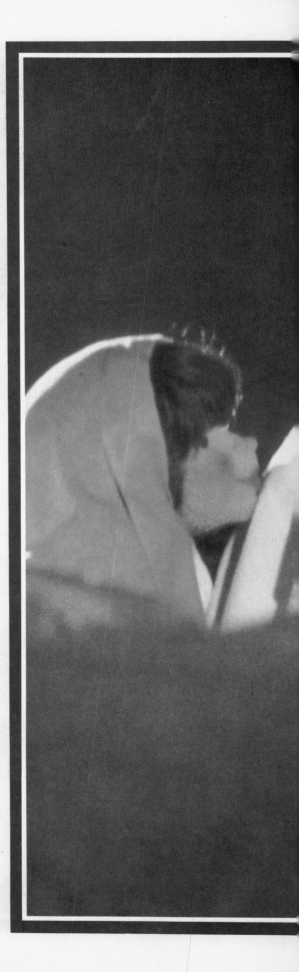

"We're looking for the right place now," added the girl. "A place where we'll feel wanted. Then we'll settle down. Maybe we'll even be servants together again."

"Hmf. Sounds like you've got it all planned. Well, here we are. Bethlehem." The shepherd gestured with his staff. "My wife and I live over that way. Not much of a town now. But it used to be pretty special. King David was born here. Ever hear of him?"

The children nodded.

"Well, this was his hometown. Folks still call it 'City of David' sometimes. Hey there! You!" He grabbed the cloak of a man who was running past. "Do you know where we can find this Baby?"

"Over there," panted the man. "In the cave behind the inn. Let me go. I have to tell my brother."

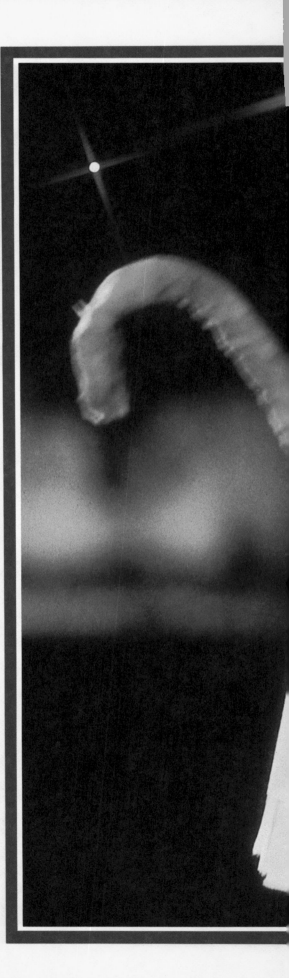

"'Cave behind the inn,' he says," grumbled the old man. "What kind of place is that for a Savior? Well, come on, you two. Stop lagging behind."

But when they got to the cave, he stopped outside as if he were afraid to go in.

"What are we waiting for?" asked the boy, hopping from foot to foot.

"Can't you let an old man catch his breath?" snapped the shepherd. "Anyway, who knows? We may not be welcome here. Dottering old man and a couple of ragamuffins."

"You are welcome," said a deep, warm voice. "Everyone is welcome here. Come in." A tall man stood at the entrance to the cave and beckoned to them. Without a word they followed him in.

"I am Joseph," said the man. "Don't worry. You're not disturbing us. This is Mary, my wife. She just fell asleep a few minutes ago. Don't worry. You won't wake her. And that's the Baby asleep on her lap. We've called Him Jesus. It's Him you've come to see, isn't it?"

They nodded silently, almost afraid to breathe. But just then the Baby looked straight at them.

"Praise God, it's true!" whispered the old shepherd. "He *is* the Savior."

The Baby waved His little hands in the air and the girl smiled.

"Hello, small Jesus," she said. "Welcome to the world." She didn't notice that tears were rolling down her face again, because deep inside her another miracle was happening. She would never be able to explain it exactly, but it was as if something cold and hard and frightened were melting. Suddenly she felt welcome too—in the cave, in the world, and in something even bigger than the world.

She turned to see if the boy was feeling the same thing. Yes, there were the tears on his face.

"May I sing Him a lullaby?" he begged. "As— as a thank You?"

"Of course," said Joseph. "He'd like that. See? He's closed His eyes already."

With shaking fingers the girl found the right notes on the recorder and then the boy began to sing:

"What Child is this, who, laid to rest,
On Mary's lap is sleeping?
Whom angels greet with anthems sweet
While shepherds watch are keeping?"

From all around them breathed the answer, soft and sure:

"This, this is Christ the King,
Whom shepherds guard and angels sing;
Haste, haste to bring Him laud,
The Babe, the Son of Mary!"

"We'll go now," said the old shepherd. He put one arm around the boy and the other around the girl. "Come, children. It's time to go home."

Once outside the cave, they stopped and stared at him.

"Home?" they said together.

"You heard me." He cleared his throat. "We've got room and my wife could use a girl to help her. Guess I could use some help too."

"Oh, sir!" The boy began jumping around with excitement. "I'd work so hard. I'd get all those pesky lambs and I'd chase away the wild animals and—and I'd sing to the sheep."

The old man smiled. "David used to do that, they say. Now remember what I told you, though. This isn't much of a place." He paused. "At least it didn't used to be. I don't know. Maybe that's all changed now. Anyway, it's your home, if you want it. You're welcome here."

Welcome. The girl felt the glad word glow inside her again. For a moment she stood, hugging its warmth. Then she put it away in her heart to keep forever.

"Thank you," she said quietly.

But the boy didn't feel at all quiet. Love and joy and the music of heaven were swelling inside him until he thought he would burst.

"One more song!" he cried and leaped onto a wall. "One more song to welcome the Stranger, the Baby who's come to save the world."

The girl's fingers were steady now as she played the tune, and the boy he shouted his song to a listening world:

"So bring Him incense, gold, and myrrh;
Come, peasant, king, to own Him.
The King of kings salvation brings.
Let loving hearts enthrone Him."

And above, the stars laughed and shouted back the refrain:

"This, this is Christ the King,
Whom shepherds guard and angels sing;
Haste, haste to bring Him laud,
The Babe, the Son of Mary!"